SALTWATER FISHING

BY KELLY ANNE WHITE

childsworld.com

The Child's World
childsworld.com

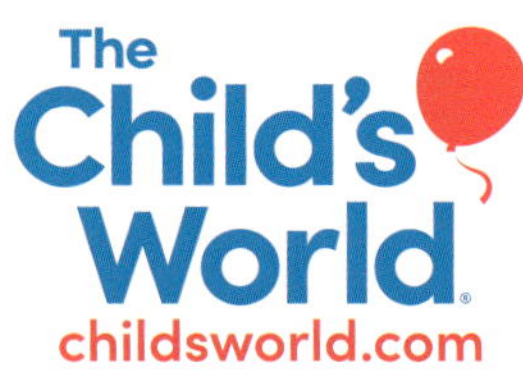

Published by The Child's World®
800-599-READ • www.childsworld.com

Photography Credits
Photographs ©: Jason Richeux/Shutterstock Images, cover, 1; HA Besen/iStockphoto, 5; Aimin Tang/iStockphoto, 6; Shutterstock Images, 7 (top left), 7 (top right), 7 (bottom middle right), 7 (bottom left), 15, 20; Hayk Shalunts/Shutterstock Images, 7 (top middle left); Valery Evlakhov/Shutterstock Images, 7 (top middle right); Jassada Watt/Shutterstock Images, 7 (bottom middle left); Luis Carlos Torres/Shutterstock Images, 7 (bottom right); iStockphoto, 9, 10, 13, 17, 21; Colin MacDonald/Shutterstock Images, 14; Martin E Doucet/iStockphoto, 19

ISBN Information
9781503869776 (Reinforced Library Binding)
9781503881044 (Portable Document Format)
9781503882355 (Online Multi-user eBook)
9781503883666 (Electronic Publication)

LCCN 2022951215

Printed in the United States of America

BRINGING THE WORLD TO YOUNG READERS 1968

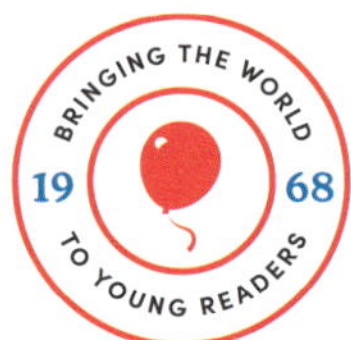

ABOUT THE AUTHOR

Kelly Anne White has written many children's books. She lives primarily in Baltimore, Maryland, and she resides part-time on Chincoteague Bay in Virginia. Both areas are rich in fish and game culture.

anythink

CONTENTS

CHAPTER ONE

Saltwater Fishing Is a Splash

Jeff and his mom pull into the beach parking lot. They get out of the truck and grab their gear. Today, they're going fishing. Jeff carries the fishing rods and **tackle** box. His mom carries a cooler and two foldable chairs. They set up in a spot where the ocean's waves are active. The waves will bring fish near the shore. This beach is Jeff's favorite fishing spot. Many **anglers** fish here. Rows of fishing rods jut out of the sand.

Jeff uses a mallet to pound two pipes into the sand. The pipes will hold the fishing rods. The rods hold fishing line. At the end of each rod's line is a metal hook. Jeff and his mom carefully **bait** their hooks with pieces of raw clam from the cooler. Then Jeff takes his rod handle and holds down a lever on the reel. The reel holds a spool of fishing line. The lever keeps the spool of line in place. The reel also has a smaller handle for pulling in the line.

When fishing from shore, anglers often use rod holders or sand spikes to keep their fishing rods in place. This way, an angler doesn't have to hold the rod while she waits for fish to bite.

Saltwater fish can be very large and heavy. To reel in these fish, many anglers use strong fishing rods designed for saltwater fishing.

Jeff raises the rod above his head. Before casting, he makes sure no one is nearby. That way, he won't accidentally hit someone. Then he snaps the rod forward. He lets go of the lever on the reel to release the line. The line flies through the air.

Thousands of fish species live in salty waters. Common types include yellowfin tuna, swordfish, blue marlin, salmon, snapper, and perch.

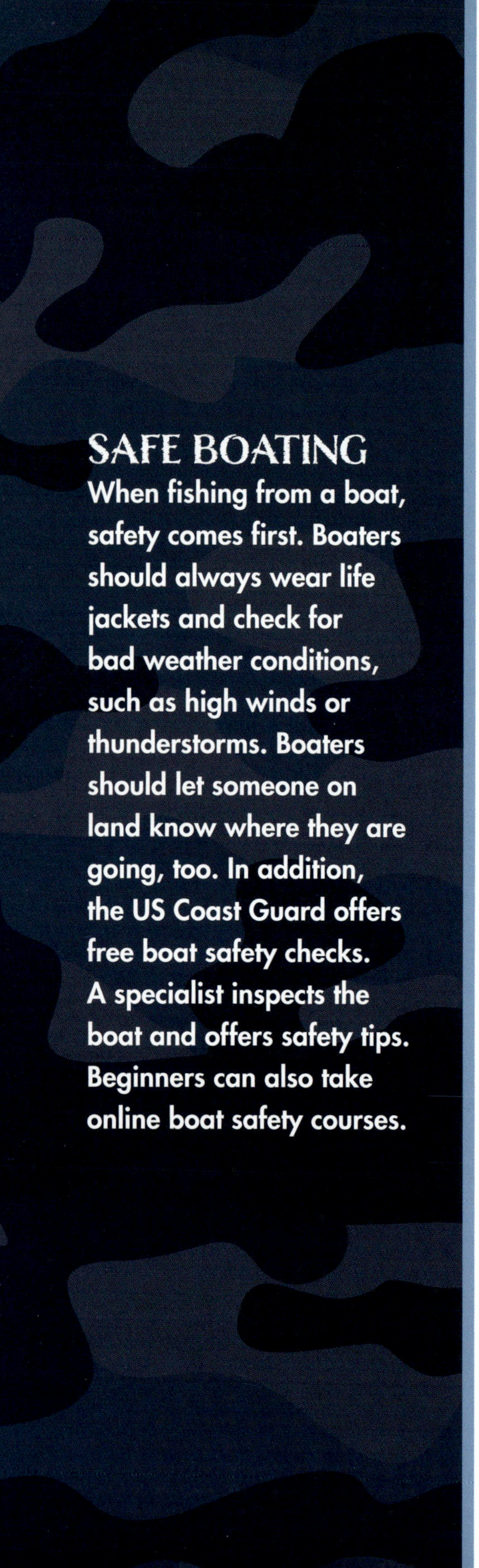

SAFE BOATING

When fishing from a boat, safety comes first. Boaters should always wear life jackets and check for bad weather conditions, such as high winds or thunderstorms. Boaters should let someone on land know where they are going, too. In addition, the US Coast Guard offers free boat safety checks. A specialist inspects the boat and offers safety tips. Beginners can also take online boat safety courses.

It lands in the ocean. Jeff slips the rod into one of the pipes in the sand. He and his mom wait patiently. They watch for tugs on their lines, which could mean fish are biting the bait.

Suddenly, Jeff's rod quivers. He grabs the rod and starts cranking the reel. After several minutes, Jeff's arms feel strained. But he keeps going. Finally, a large fish breaks through the waves. Jeff has hooked a flounder!

Sometimes Jeff and his mom eat the fish they catch. But today Jeff will let the flounder go. This is called catch and release. Jeff uses pliers to quickly remove the hook from the flounder's mouth. This helps him avoid tearing or damaging the fish's mouth.

Jeff also uses a ruler to measure the fish. Most anglers try to catch big fish. The flounder is 20 inches (51 cm), which is a good length. Jeff writes down the length in his fishing log. Then he releases the fish back into the waves.

Trolling is a popular fishing method. Anglers attach fishing rods to their boats and let them drag behind in the water. They set up several fishing rods in a row to attract more fish.

Like Jeff, many anglers enjoy fishing in oceans, seas, bays, and **gulfs**. These bodies of water have a high **salinity**. Some fish species survive only in salt water. This is because they have very high levels of salt in their bodies. Some fish, such as salmon and eels, are found in both fresh water and salt water.

Many fishing piers are located near beaches and boardwalks. Anglers can find different fish in these areas depending on the tides, water conditions, and time of day.

Many saltwater anglers fish in saltwater channels and straits. Straits are narrow bodies of water that connect two larger bodies of water. Channels are wide straits located between two areas of land. Saltwater anglers often fish where two bodies of water meet because fish gather in those places.

Some saltwater anglers prefer surf fishing, or fishing from shore. Others fish from a pier or jetty. A jetty is a long structure made of stone or concrete. It extends from the land into a body of water. A jetty can offer fish an ideal habitat to gather away from the tides. Habitats are places where plants and animals live. Jetties provide fish with many places to rest or hide. Fish can also find food around jetties.

Some anglers fish from boats, too. Fishing from a boat far out on the water is called offshore fishing. Anglers can use many kinds of boats for fishing. In smaller, calmer bodies of salt water, many people fish from canoes and kayaks. Larger, sturdier boats are needed for deep-sea fishing. Deep-sea fishing happens offshore, far out on the ocean. Anglers can catch larger fish such as marlin or tuna when deep-sea fishing. These fish can weigh hundreds of pounds. Because of this, deep-sea fishing requires heavy-duty equipment. This includes longer fishing rods, thicker fishing line, and stronger hooks.

CHAPTER TWO

Saltwater Fishing Basics

Before going saltwater fishing, anglers should be prepared. Every angler needs a saltwater fishing license. This gives an angler permission to fish. People can buy fishing licenses online or at outdoor sports stores. Many states allow kids under 16 years old to fish without a license. To stay safe, kids should fish with an experienced adult.

Anglers must pay a fee to get a fishing license. The money goes to state agencies that manage wildlife. The agencies put the money toward fish **conservation**. Many states also offer free fishing days. On these days, anglers can fish without a license.

Each state has its own fishing regulations. Many states set rules about where and when anglers can fish. For example, some public waters don't allow fishing. Fishing seasons determine the months when anglers are allowed to catch certain fish. Usually, fish species with stable populations may be caught year-round. Some states also have rules about which fishing gear is allowed.

Deep-sea anglers should follow all boat safety guidelines, such as wearing life jackets.

Fish such as swordfish, marlin (pictured), and sharks are highly migratory species. This means they travel long distances across oceans. Anglers need special permits to fish for these species.

Fishing nets, for example, are banned at specific times of the year. This is because nets could catch other marine animals, such as turtles, that are in the waters during certain seasons.

Saltwater anglers also need the right gear. The most important tool for saltwater fishing is a fishing rod. Saltwater fishing rods are usually made of materials such as **graphite** or **fiberglass**.

An angler's fishing supplies are known as tackle. Most anglers store smaller tackle items, such as fishing line, in tackle boxes. Fishing line is usually made of **nylon** and comes on a spool. The line is cut from the spool. It is then tied to the reel and threaded along the rod.

Some anglers wear fishing belts or harnesses. These help anglers reel in heavy fish that fight and pull on the line.

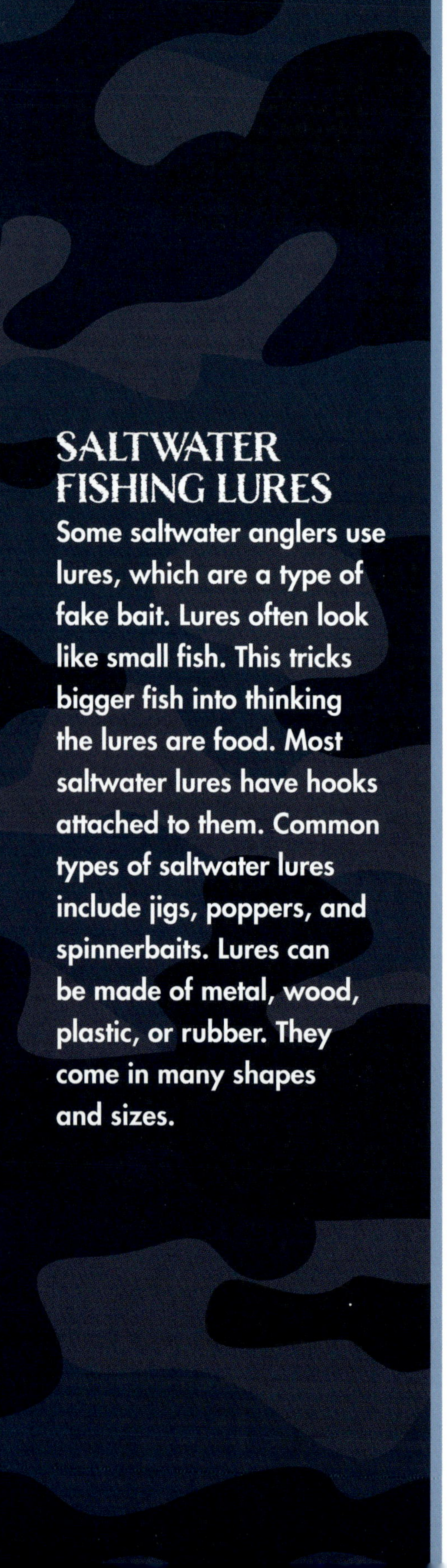

SALTWATER FISHING LURES

Some saltwater anglers use lures, which are a type of fake bait. Lures often look like small fish. This tricks bigger fish into thinking the lures are food. Most saltwater lures have hooks attached to them. Common types of saltwater lures include jigs, poppers, and spinnerbaits. Lures can be made of metal, wood, plastic, or rubber. They come in many shapes and sizes.

Hooks and sinkers are also kept in tackle boxes. Anglers tie hooks and sinkers to the end of fishing lines. Saltwater sinkers are small and usually made of lead. They add weight to the fishing line so it sinks in the water. Saltwater hooks are usually made of steel. They come in various shapes and sizes. The best choice of hook depends on the type of fish being caught and the type of bait used. Catch-and-release anglers use special hooks that are less likely to injure fish.

Bait is also important. Some saltwater anglers use live bait, such as crabs and small fish, to attract larger fish. Live bait must be kept alive. It is usually stored in a bucket of water. Other bait includes raw clams, mussels, shrimp, or squid. These types of bait are usually not alive. They are kept on ice in a cooler when not being used.

Many saltwater anglers use brightly colored lures such as jigs, poppers, and spinnerbaits. These lures resemble marine animals such as small fish, squid, or shrimp.

Other fishing supplies include pliers and line cutters. These tools are used for removing hooks from fish and cutting catches from the line. Anglers fishing for food may also use buckets to keep fish in water until they can be prepared for a meal.

CHAPTER THREE

Getting Started

Getting started with saltwater fishing takes time and practice. Anglers must learn several skills, such as how to tie knots in fishing line. Fishing line must be properly tied to the reel. This keeps the line from snapping off when anglers reel in fish. Anglers should also learn special knots for tying hooks and sinkers to their lines. These knots must be secure. This way, the hooks and sinkers don't come loose. There are hundreds of knots to choose from.

Beginners should also practice baiting hooks, casting lines, and reeling in catches. They should learn how to safely remove fish from hooks, too. Kids can take fishing lessons or join clubs to practice their skills.

Anglers should follow all fishing rules in their area. Many anglers practice catch and release. Others turn their catches into meals or display fish as trophies in their homes. Whether fishing for food or sport, anglers typically measure their catches. In some states, fish must meet a size limit in order for anglers to keep them. Smaller fish must be released so they can grow and reproduce.

Kids and beginners can practice their saltwater fishing skills with experienced anglers.

For some fish species, there are also limits to how many anglers can keep. Sometimes anglers can keep only one fish per day of a certain species. This rule applies to species such as rockfish, whose populations are falling in some regions. The limit keeps the population from becoming too small. When fishing for food, anglers should never keep more fish than they can eat.

Some anglers go on fishing trips with experienced guides, who help them learn new techniques and improve their skills.

Anglers who plan to eat their catches should learn how to properly prepare and clean fish. This helps keep the fish fresh.

If an angler plans to eat the fish he catches, he must prepare it properly. To prepare a fish, the angler must first clean it. This involves cutting off the fish's head and removing its insides.

Saltwater fishing is a fun, exciting sport. But responsible anglers also take saltwater fishing seriously, especially when it comes to safety. It's important for people to respect fish and anglers around them. This makes saltwater fishing enjoyable for everyone.

GLOSSARY

anglers (AN-gluhrz) Anglers are people who fish with a line and hook. Saltwater anglers fish for species such as snappers, swordfish, and groupers.

bait (BAYT) To bait a fishing hook is to put food on the hook to attract fish. Some saltwater anglers bait their hooks with shellfish or small fish.

conservation (kon-sur-VAY-shuhn) Conservation is the protection of wildlife and other natural resources. Anglers can support fish conservation by following state fishing rules.

fiberglass (FYE-buhr-glas) Fiberglass is a material made of glass fibers. Fiberglass fishing rods are a good choice for beginners because they are sturdy and inexpensive.

graphite (GRAH-fyte) Graphite is a material made mainly of carbon fibers. Graphite fishing rods are better for more experienced anglers.

gulfs (GULFS) Gulfs are bodies of salt water that extend into land from the ocean or sea. Many saltwater anglers fish in gulfs, bays, and coves.

nylon (NYE-lon) Nylon is a plastic material used to make many products, including fishing line. Many anglers like nylon fishing line because it is stretchy and strong.

salinity (suh-LIH-nuh-tee) Salinity refers to the level of salt in water, soil, and other substances. Bodies of salt water have very high salinity.

tackle (TAK-uhl) Tackle includes any equipment or gear that anglers use when fishing. Common fishing tackle items include rods, reels, hooks, lines, and sinkers.

FAST FACTS

- Many saltwater anglers fish in seas, gulfs, bays, and coves. They can fish from shore or by boat. Saltwater anglers fish for species such as groupers, swordfish, and snappers.
- Each state has its own rules about when and where anglers are allowed to fish. Anglers should follow all fishing rules in their area.
- A saltwater angler's most important tools are a good rod and reel.
- A tackle box holds an angler's supplies. Items such as hooks, sinkers, and fishing line are useful to have in a tackle box.
- Anglers use bait to attract fish. Some saltwater anglers prefer live or raw bait, while others use artificial lures.
- Some saltwater anglers fish for sport, catching fish and then releasing them. Others fish for food. Saltwater anglers who fish for food should keep only as much as they can eat.

ONE STRIDE FURTHER

- If you were to go saltwater fishing, would you keep fish to eat? Or would you practice catch and release? Explain your choice.
- Imagine you are going on a fishing trip by boat. Make a safety checklist for your trip. What supplies will you bring?
- Write an ad for a make-believe fishing club. Describe the saltwater fishing skills that people will learn in the club. Why is it important for anglers to learn these skills?

FIND OUT MORE

IN THE LIBRARY

Kingston, Seth. *Fishing*. New York, NY: PowerKids Press, 2022.

Lisi, David. *Fishing Logbook for Kids: Observe and Record Your Catches*. Emeryville, CA: Rockridge Press, 2021.

Mazzarella, Kerri. *Deep Sea Fishing*. New York, NY: Crabtree, 2023.

ON THE WEB

Visit our website for links about saltwater fishing:
childsworld.com/links

Note to Parents, Caregivers, Teachers, and Librarians: We routinely verify our Web links to make sure they are safe and active sites. So encourage your readers to check them out!

INDEX